new edition

English network

Pocket Grammar B1

Gaynor Ramsey und Simon Tribe
mit Lynda Hübner

Langenscheidt

Berlin · Madrid · München · Warschau · Wien · Zürich

English Network Pocket Grammar B1

Autoren:
Gaynor Ramsey, Simon Tribe mit Lynda Hübner

Beratung:
Lynda Hübner

Redaktion:
Helge Sturmfels

Grafik und Layout:
Design Im Kontor – Iris Steiner, München, Gestaltungskonzept und Layout
Kaltnermedia, Bobingen, Satz und Layout
Sabine Nasko, München, Umschlag

Symbole:
\+ = bejahter Satz, Aussagesatz
– = verneinter Satz
? = Fragesatz

www.langenscheidt.de/englishnetwork

Druck und Bindung: Stürtz GmbH, Würzburg
ISBN 978-3-526-50514-3

09041

Wegweiser

Welcome to *English Network Pocket Grammar B1*! Mit diesem Buch können Sie Ihre Kenntnisse der englischen Grammatik schnell und effektiv auffrischen. Der Band enthält die wichtigsten Grammatikbereiche der Stufe B1 des *Gemeinsamen europäischen Referenzrahmens für Sprachen* und hilft Ihnen, Ihre Grammatiklücken zu schließen.

English Network Pocket Grammar B1 soll in erster Linie eine Übungsgrammatik sein. Unser Ziel ist es daher, den jeweiligen Grammatikbereich kurz und prägnant zu erklären und Ihnen genügend Möglichkeit zum vertiefenden Üben zu geben.

Um den größtmöglichen Lernerfolg zu sichern, sind die Grammatikbereiche in einer besonderen Weise angeordnet:

Teil A: Hier finden Sie die wichtigen eigenständigen Grammatikphänomene: So gibt es z.B. einen eigenen Abschnitt zu *Present simple* und einen weiteren zu *Present progressive*. Jedes Thema wird anschaulich erklärt, Sie erhalten Hinweise zu den Formen, zum Gebrauch und zu Besonderheiten des jeweiligen Bereichs. Über eine anschließende Übung zur Formenbildung können Sie dann überprüfen, ob Sie alles richtig verstanden haben. Von Teil A aus erhalten Sie aber auch konkrete Hinweise, mit welchen Grammatikbereichen Sie sich nun sinnvollerweise beschäftigen sollten. Diese Verweise führen Sie zu den entsprechenden Seiten in ...

Teil B: Hier geht es darum, Sie im Gebrauch kombinierter oder weiterführender Grammatikphänomene sicher zu machen: So werden nun z.B. *Present simple* und *Present progressive* zusammen behandelt, damit Sie wissen, wann Sie welche Zeitform verwenden sollten. Sie erhalten zunächst Erläuterungen mit prägnanten Beispielsätzen, die wichtige Unterschiede oft anschaulicher darstellen als lange Erklärungen. Daran schließen sich dann wieder Übungen an, damit Sie fit in der Anwendung der Grammatik werden.

Am Ende des Buches finden Sie einen Lösungsschlüssel zu allen Übungen im Buch, eine Liste mit den deutschen Entsprechungen der im Buch verwendeten englischen Grammatikbegriffe und zwei alphabetische Register, die alle englischen bzw. deutschen Grammatikbegriffe mit Seitenzahlen aufführen. Auf der vorderen und der hinteren Umschlaginnenseite befinden sich zusätzlich Übersichten mit wichtigen unregelmäßigen Verben.

Ob zu Hause oder unterwegs – mit *English Network Pocket Grammar B1* haben Sie Ihre Englischgrammatik fest im Griff.

Viel Spaß und Erfolg wünschen Ihnen

Gaynor Ramsey, Simon Tribe, Lynda Hübner

Gaynor Ramsey, Simon Tribe, Lynda Hübner
und Ihr Langenscheidt ELT Verlag

Inhalt

Inhalt

Inhalt

Present simple

- Die **einfache Gegenwart** bezeichnet gewohnheitsmäßige, sich wiederholende Handlungen.
- Sie wird auch in Aussagen verwendet, die allgemein gültig sind.

How **do you go** to the office?	**I walk** there.	But **I don't walk** home.
Where **does he/she work**?	**He/She works** in ...	But **he/she doesn't work** in ...
Where **do you live**?	**We live** in ...	But **we don't live** in ...
What **do they learn** at school?	**They** all **learn** ...	But **they don't** all **learn** ...

- **Wichtig** "He / She / It – das 's' muss mit." In der 3. Person Singular wird ein *-s* an das Ende des Verbs angehängt *(work ▸ works)*, *do* wird zu *does* und *don't* zu *doesn't*.
- **Rechtschreibung** Wenn *-y* auf einen Konsonanten folgt, wird in der 3. Person Singular *-y* zu *-ies*: *try ▸ tries*. Wenn das Verb auf *-sh* oder *-ch* endet, wird in der 3. Person Singular *-es* angehängt: *wash ▸ washes*.

1 Cross out the wrong word.

1 I usually *take* / ~~*takes*~~ the bus. It always ~~*arrive*~~ / *arrives* on time. **2** The shops *open* / ~~*opens*~~ at 9 on weekdays. **3** We *like* / ~~*likes*~~ getting up late on Sundays. **4** What time ~~*do*~~ / *does* Jane *start* / ~~*starts*~~ work? **5** She ~~*finish*~~ / *finishes* at 6.30. **6** She ~~*don't*~~ / *doesn't* have much free time. **7** *Do* / ~~*Does*~~ you like olives? – I *don't* / ~~*doesn't*~~.

2 Write in the correct form of the verbs in brackets.

1 Kim (+ eat) .... there every day. **2** Jim (+ wash) .... his new car once a week. **3** (? get up) .... Susan .... early in the morning? **4** Tom (– like) ...doesn't... .... his job. **5** We (+ do) .... yoga every morning. **6** No, I (– know) .... where he is. **7** She always (+ try) .... to be at the office before her boss arrives. **8** How often (? watch) .... you .... TV in the evenings? **9** She (+ try) .... to be punctual but she sometimes (+ come) .... late.

S. 51

Present progressive

A

- Die **Verlaufsform der Gegenwart** wird verwendet, um über Dinge zu sprechen, die im Moment geschehen.
- Sie wird ebenfalls benutzt, wenn etwas in einem Zeitraum geschieht, der noch nicht abgeschlossen ist, z.B. *today, this week: We're learning about the present tenses this week.*

What **are you reading**?	**I am reading** my book.	**I'm not reading** the paper.
What **is he/she doing**?	**He/She is talking** to ...	**He/She isn't reading.**
What **are you** two **talking** about?	**We are talking** about our ...	**We aren't talking** about ...
What **are they doing** today?	**They are doing** tests all day.	**They aren't having** lessons.

- **Rechtschreibung** *swim ▸ swimming, take ▸ taking, lie ▸ lying.*

Rewrite these sentences. Change them according to what you can see in brackets.

1 She's learning French.

(I / –) ....

(you / ?) ....

(they / +) ....

2 Are they working today?

(they / –) ....

(he / –) ....

(he / ?) ....

S. 51

Present progressive

Stative verbs 27

Present simple and **present progressive** 28

Present perfect simple

A

- Die **einfache Form der vollendeten Gegenwart** wird mit *have / has* und dem Partizip der Vergangenheit des Verbs (*drunk / eaten* usw.) gebildet.
- Sie wird verwendet, um Aussagen über das gesamte Leben einer Person bis zur Gegenwart zu machen (A), und auch um über einen unvollendeten Zeitraum zu sprechen, z.B. *this week, today* (B).
- **Häufige Signalwörter:** *just, already, not yet, yet* (C).
- Sie wird auch verwendet, um Handlungen zu beschreiben, die zu einem unbestimmten oder ungenannten Zeitpunkt in der Vergangenheit stattgefunden haben (D).

A	**Have you ever been** to Paris?	**I've been** to France.	**I've never been** to Paris.
B	**Has he seen** her this week?	**He's phoned** her.	**He hasn't seen** her.
C	**Have you planned** your holiday yet?	**I've already chosen** the hotel. **I've just booked** it.	**I haven't reserved** the flights yet.
D	**She has found** a new job, **has sold** her house and **has moved** to Scotland.		

Write in the correct form of the verbs in brackets, and complete the short answers.

1 (open / yet) ………… the new restaurant ………………………………… ? – No, it …hasn't… , but they (already / finish) …………have already finished… building it. **2** (happen) ……Has anything interesting …happened……… this week? **3** (have / yet) ……Have you ……had…… dinner ………… ? Then come over to my place. I (just / order) ……………………………… a large pizza. **4** (ever / try) …………… you ……………………… sushi? – Yes, I …………… .

S. 51

Present perfect simple
Present simple and **present perfect simple** 28
Present perfect simple and present perfect progressive 29
Past simple and **present perfect simple** 30

Present perfect progressive

A

- Die **Verlaufsform der vollendeten Gegenwart** wird für Aktivitäten verwendet, die in der Vergangenheit begonnen wurden und bis in die Gegenwart andauern. Sie wird gebildet aus der vollendeten Gegenwart von *to be (have / has been)* und der *ing*-Form des Hauptverbs.

How long **have you been reading** the newspaper?	**I have been reading** it since breakfast.	**I haven't been reading** it for more than an hour.
How long **has he/she been working** …?	**He/She has been working …**	**He/She hasn't been working …**
How long **have you been learning** …?	**We have been learning …**	**We haven't been learning …**
How long **have they been living** here?	**They have been living …**	**They haven't been living …**

- Die **Verlaufsform der vollendeten Gegenwart** wird häufig mit ***since*** + einer genauen Zeitangabe in der Vergangenheit (z.B. *breakfast*) oder mit ***for*** + einer Zeitdauer (z.B. *more than an hour*) gebraucht.

Write in the correct form of the verbs in brackets an choose between *for* and *since* in 1 and 5.

1 Tim (+ look) ……………… ……………… ……………………………… for a new flat *for/since* months.

2 How long (? live) ……………… the Johnsons ……………… ……………………………… in that house?

3 Please come in, I hope you (– wait) ……………………… ……………… ……………………………… long.

4 Dave looks tired. I think he (+ work) ……………… ……………… ……………………………… too hard.

5 Ann (+ learn) ……………… ……………… ……………………………… Chinese *for/since* she was 18.

6 John (– get) ……………………… ……………… ……………………………………… much exercise lately.

S. 51

Present perfect progressive
Present simple and **present perfect progressive** 30
Present perfect simple and **present perfect progressive** 29

Past simple

A

- Die **einfache Vergangenheit** wird verwendet, um von etwas zu sprechen, das zu einem bestimmten Zeitpunkt in der Vergangenheit stattgefunden hat.
- Die Verbformen sind in allen Personen identisch (Ausnahme: *to be* = *was / were*).

Where **were you/they** yesterday?	**I was** at home. **We/They were** at home.	**I wasn't** at work. **We/They weren't** at work.
Where **was he/she** on Sunday?	**He/She was** in London..	**He/She wasn't** at home.
How **did you/he/she/they go** home?	**I/He/She/We/They went** home by taxi.	**I/He/She/We/They didn't go** home by train.

Write in the correct form of the verbs in brackets, and complete the short answers.

1 What (? do) .... you .... in Paris? – I (+ visit) .... an old friend of mine there. **2** (? be) .... you there long? – No, I only (+ stay) .... for the weekend. **3** (? go) .... you .... by train? – No, I (+ fly) .... **4** (? see) .... you .... the Mona Lisa in the Louvre? – No, I .... , but we (+ go) .... up the Eiffel Tower. **5** I bet the food was good. – Yes, it (+ be) .... We (+ eat) .... dinner in a charming little bistro and (+ drink) .... an espresso or two afterwards.

S. 51

Past simple

Used to	31
Past simple and present perfect simple	30
Past simple and past progressive	32
Past simple and past perfect simple	32
Past simple and past perfect progressive	33

Past progressive

A

- Die **Verlaufsform der Vergangenheit** wird verwendet, um über Handlungen zu sprechen, die während eines bestimmten Zeitraums in der Vergangenheit stattgefunden haben.
- Sie wird oft benutzt, um den zeitlichen Hintergrund auszudrücken und beschreibt, was zu einem Zeitpunkt in der Vergangenheit gerade passierte oder was jemand gerade tat.

What **were you doing** at 8 a.m.?	**I was having** breakfast.	**I wasn't working** at 8.
What **was he/she doing** when the phone rang?	**He/She was watching** TV.	**He/She wasn't having** dinner.
What **were you** two **doing** when he arrived?	**We were sitting** in the garden.	**We weren't waiting** for him in the house.
What **were they doing** when the fire alarm rang?	**They were learning** English.	**They weren't having** a coffee break.

What was happening at the time? Write in the correct form of the verbs in brackets.

1 This time last year Kim (+ travel) .... in Asia. She (– work) .... 2 (? jog) .... Dave .... yesterday at 4 p.m.? – No, it (+ rain) .... 3 The kids (+ party) .... still .... when their parents came home. 4 (+ ride) He .... his bike when the police stopped him. He (– wear) .... a helmet. 5 (? lie) .... you .... on the beach when the rain started? – No, I (+ write) .... cards at the hotel.

S. 51

Past progressive — Past simple and **past progressive** 32

Past perfect simple

A

- Wenn wir über etwas Vergangenes sprechen, verwenden wir die einfache Vergangenheit. Wenn wir ausdrücken wollen, dass etwas noch vor dieser Zeit passierte, verwenden wir die vollendete Vergangenheit.
- Die **einfache Form der vollendeten Vergangenheit** wird mit *had* + dem Partizip der Vergangenheit (*gone / seen / taken*, etc.) gebildet.
- Die Verbformen sind in allen Personen identisch.

Had you already **seen** that film before it was on TV last week?	Yes, **I had** already **seen** it twice.	But **I hadn't seen** it in English.

Write in the correct form of the verbs in brackets and complete the short forms.

1 When Bill arrived, the meeting (+ finish) .... already .... 2 She was starving when the food arrived. She (– eat) .... anything all day. 3 I was at the opera yesterday. – (? be) .... you .... before ? – No, I .... 4 Kim went to her school reunion. Some of her friends (+ change) .... a lot. 5 Tom thought that he (+ put) .... the film in the camera, but afterwards he realised that he .... 6 Jamie had a skiing accident, but the doctors later said he (– break) .... any bones.

S. 51

Past perfect simple — Past simple and **past perfect simple** 32
Past perfect simple and past perfect progressive 33

Past perfect progressive

A

- Die **Verlaufsform der vollendeten Vergangenheit** wird für Handlungen verwendet, die in der Vergangenheit bis zu einem bestimmten Zeitpunkt stattgefunden haben, an dem etwas anderes passierte.
- Sie wird gebildet mit *had* + *been* + der *ing*-Form des Verbs: *had been living*.
- Die Verformen sind in allen Personen identisch.

How long **had you been waiting** when she arrived?	**I had been waiting** for ten minutes.	**I hadn't been waiting** too long.

- Die **Verlaufsform der vollendeten Vergangenheit** wird häufig mit ***since*** + einer genauen Zeitangabe in der Vergangenheit (z.B. *breakfast*) oder mit ***for*** + einer Zeitdauer (z.B. *ten minutes*) gebraucht.

What had these people been doing? Write in the correct form of the verbs in brackets and complete the short answers.

1 I (+ sit) .... in the waiting room for an hour before my number was called. **2** The lorry driver (– drive) .... very long before he had the accident. **3** (? miss) .... they .... long when the rescue team found them? – No, they .... **4** (? work) .... the new boss .... there long when he was fired? – Yes, he .... **5** They (+ try) .... to solve the problem for weeks before they found a solution. **6** How long (? write) .... you .... e-mails when your computer crashed? **7** (? negotiate) .... the executives .... long before they agreed? – Yes, they ....

S. 51

Past perfect progressive

Past simple and **past perfect progressive** 33
Past perfect simple and **past perfect progressive** 33

Future simple

A

- Die **Zukunft mit *will*** wird verwendet, um über Tatsachen zu sprechen: *I'll be in Paris this time next week.*
- Sie wird auch für spontane Entscheidungen verwendet: *I think I'll stay at home this evening.*
- Ebenso kann ein Angebot damit ausgedrückt werden: *I'll bring the wine to the party.*
- Und auch für Vermutungen kann diese Zeitform verwendet werden: *There'll probably be about fifty people at the party.*
- Die Verbformen sind in allen Personen identisch: *will* (Aussage), *won't* (Verneinung).

Where **will you be** on Friday?	**I'll be** in London.	**I won't be** at home.
How many people will there be at the party?	I think **there'll be** about fifty.	**There won't be** more than sixty.

- **Wichtig** Die Kurzform von *will ('ll)* wird normalerweise in Aussagesätzen verwendet, nicht aber in Fragen oder Antworten. *Won't (will not)* wird immer verwendet, außer in sehr dramatischen Situationen mit der Betonung auf *not: No, I will **not** work on Friday!*

Write the correct form of these verbs in the gaps and complete the short answers.

bring | be | carry | cost | finish | make | phone

1 Would you like to come over later and watch the match? - Sure, I .... the beer.

2 Do you think they .... the project on time? – Yes, I'm sure they ....

3 Julie, you look tired. – You're right. I need a break. I think I .... a cup of coffee.

4 .... the boss .... at the meeting? – No, she .... , but she .... us later.

5 Those boxes are really heavy. Don't lift them by yourself. I .... them for you.

6 They have invited 300 guests to their wedding. I'm sure it .... a fortune.

S. 51

Future simple
Future simple and future progressive 34
Future simple and future perfect 35

Future with *going to*

A

- Die **Zukunft mit *going to*** wird verwendet, um über Pläne und Absichten zu sprechen.
- Sie wird auch für unmittelbar bevorstehende Ereignisse verwendet: Wenn Sie z.B. einen Kellner mit einer Speisekarte auf sich zukommen sehen, könnten Sie sagen: *He's going to give me the menu.*

What **are you going to do** in the summer? **I/We are going to stay** at home.
Is she going to give a New Year party? No, **she isn't going to celebrate** it at home this year.
What **are they going to do** on their wedding anniversary? **They're going to invite** their children out for dinner.

- **Wichtig** Die Formen *going to go* und *going to come* klingen nicht besonders gut. Sie sind nicht falsch, werden aber normalerweise verkürzt zu ***I'm going*** ~~*to go*~~ *to London next week*, ***I'm*** ~~*going to come*~~ *home on Friday.* ► ***I'm coming*** *home on Friday.*

Complete the sentences using the future with *going to.*

1 When (? get married) .... they ....?

2 What (? wear) .... the bride ....?

3 They (– marry) .... in a church.

4 Who (? take) .... the photos?

5 They (+ go) .... Bermuda for their honeymoon.

S. 51 6 I (+ throw) .... a lot of confetti.

Future with *going to*	
Future with *going to* and future with present progressive	35
Was going to	36

Future with present simple

A

- Die **Zukunft mit der einfachen Gegenwart** (siehe auch Seite 7) wird mit Bezug auf Fahr- und Zeitpläne eher offizieller Art verwendet.

My friends are coming to visit me on Saturday. Their bus **arrives** here at 3.30. We want to go to the cinema. The film **starts** at 7.30 and **ends** at 9.15, so we'll have time after that to have a drink – their bus home **leaves** at about 11 o'clock.

Complete the sentences with the present simple form of these verbs:
close | change | finish | go | land | run | take off

1 My flight to Berlin .... at 9.40 and it .... one hour later. 2 Our English lesson .... in twenty minutes. 3 Our local shop .... at 10 p.m. tonight. 4 Wintertime .... to summertime next week. 5 The soldiers .... on parade in twenty

S. 51 minutes. 6 The all-night buses .... till 6 a.m.

Future with present simple	
When, as soon as, etc.	37

Future with present progressive

A

- Die **Zukunft mit der Verlaufsform der Gegenwart** (siehe auch Seite 8) kann für feste Vereinbarungen verwendet werden.

What time **are you** all **meeting** tomorrow?	**I'm meeting** Bob at 6.30.	**We're not meeting** Pat till later.

- Dieser Gebrauch der **Verlaufsform der Gegenwart** wird manchmal *diary tense* genannt, da er oft feste Vereinbarungen mit anderen Menschen beschreibt, wie den Kauf einer Eintrittskarte, die Vereinbarung eines Termins oder eine Reservierung usw. – Dinge, die man in einen Kalender eintragen würde.

Write in the correct form of the verbs in brackets and complete the short answers.

1 Lisa (+ play) .... tennis on Friday. **2** We (+ have) .... a party tonight. (? come) .... you ....? – Yes, I .... **3** When (? leave) .... we .... for the airport? **4** (? work) .... you both .... next week? – I ...., but Sue .... **5** (? do) .... you .... anything this afternoon? – Yes, I .... At 3.30 I (+ go) .... to the doctor's. **6** (? fly) .... they .... to Scotland? – No, they ...., they (+ drive) ....

S. 51

Future with present progressive — Future with *going to* and **future with present progressive** 35

Future progressive

A

- Die **Verlaufsform der Zukunft mit *will*** wird für Handlungen verwendet, die zu einem bestimmten Zeitpunkt in der Zukunft begonnen haben und noch andauern werden.
- Sie wird gebildet mit *will* + *be* + der *ing*-Form des Verbs: *will be working*.
- Die Verbformen sind in allen Personen identisch.

What job **will you be doing** ten years from now?	Maybe **I'll be working** for the same company.	But **I won't be working** in the same position.

What will these people be doing? Write in the correct form of the verbs in brackets.

1 The Queen (+ visit) ………… ………… …………………………………… Paris on Tuesday. She (– arrive) ………………… ……………… ……………………………………… before evening. How long (+ stay) ……………… she ………… ………………………… ?

2 At 6 a.m. I (+ sleep) ………… still ………… ……………………………… . I (– get up) ……………………………… ………………… ……………………………………… then. I (+ dream) …………………… probably ……………………… ……………………………………………… .

3 What (? do) ………… you ………… ………………… on the course? They (+ show) ………… ………… ……………………………… us new software. We (– have) ………… ………… ……………………………… much fun!

S. 51

Future progressive
Future simple and **future progressive** 34
Future progressive and future perfect 37

Future perfect

A

- Die **vollendete Zukunft** wird für Handlungen verwendet, die zu einer bestimmten Zeit in der Zukunft abgeschlossen sein werden.
- Sie wird gebildet mit *will* + *have* + dem Partizip der Vergangenheit: *will have written.*
- Die Verbformen sind in allen Personen identisch.

When **will you have finished** your work?	**I'll have written** the agenda by lunchtime.	But **I won't have** sent the mails by then.

- Die **vollendete Zukunft** wird häufig mit ***by*** + einer genauen Zeitangabe in der Zukunft benutzt: *I'll have completed this course by Christmas.*

Write in the correct form of the verbs in brackets.

1 In July she (+ have) ……………………………………………… her car for over 10 years. **2** (? finish) ………………… you ………………………………………………………… cooking when the first guests arrive? **3** No, the engineers (– find) ………………………………………………………… a solution by this afternoon. **4** She (+ swim) ……………………………………………… fifty lengths by the end of her training session. **5** I hope we (– spend) ……………………………………………………… all our money before the holiday starts. **6** (? give) ………… they ……………………………………………… her a pay rise by June?

S. 51

Future perfect
Future simple and **future perfect** 35
Future progressive and **future perfect** 37

Gerunds and Infinitives

A

- Der **Infinitiv** (*to* ...) wird nach bestimmten Verben verwendet (A).
- Das **Gerund** (*ing*-Form) wird ebenfalls nach bestimmten Verben verwendet (B).
- Es wird auch nach bestimmten Wortfügungen verwendet (C).
- Ebenso kann es nach Präpositionen stehen (D).

A	**decide, plan, promise, offer, want**	I **want to go** there.
B	**dislike, enjoy, finish, miss, suggest**	He **finished writing** the report.
C	**I feel like ..., I can't bear ..., I can't stand ..., I don't mind ..., It's no use ...**	I can't **bear wearing** a tie.
D	**thank someone for ..., be keen on ..., be fond of ..., be interested in ..., be good/bad at ...,**	I **thanked** him **for watering** my plants.

- **Wichtig!** In der Wortfügung *looking forward to* ist *to* eine Präposition und nicht Teil des Infinitivs. Daher schließt sich daran ein Gerund an: *We **are looking forward to seeing** you on Monday.*

Complete the sentences with the gerund or infinitive form of the verb in brackets.

1 I suggest (reserve) .... a table. **2** He offered (drive) .... me to the airport. **3** She's not very keen on (go) .... to the opera. **4** Thank you very much for (look after) .... my cats. **5** Are you good at (make) .... cocktails? **6** They decided (fly) .... to Berlin. **7** I don't mind (help) .... you with your application. **8** I'm sorry, I can't promise (be) .... on time.

S. 51

Gerunds and infinitives — **Gerunds and infinitives:** *stop, remember, try* 38

Have something done – present and past

A

- Mit ***have something done*** können Sie ausdrücken, dass jemand anderes etwas für Sie macht – normalerweise gegen Bezahlung oder von Berufs wegen.

I **have my hair cut** every six weeks.
I **had my hair cut** yesterday. – Where **did** you **have it cut**?
He **has his car cleaned** once a month, but he **didn't have it cleaned** last month – he did it himself.

- **Wichtig** Die Satzstellung ist sehr wichtig: *I have my windows cleaned* = Jemand anderes macht es. *I have cleaned my windows* = Ich habe es selbst gemacht.

Write these words in the correct order.

1 my always groceries I delivered have ……………………………………………… **2** house year she painted her had last ……………………………………………… **3** done has for he him washing usually his ……………………………………………… **4** month we built last had garage a ………………………………………………

5 their cut regularly they grass have ……………………………………………… **6** last we decorated bedrooms had year our all ………………………………………………

S. 51

Have something done – present and past —— *Have something done* – mixed tenses 38

The passive – present and past

A

- Das **Passiv der einfachen Gegenwart** wird mit der einfachen Gegenwart von *to be (is / are)* und dem Partizip der Vergangenheit des Hauptverbs gebildet, z.B. *driven, seen.*
- Das **Passiv der einfachen Vergangenheit** wird mit der einfachen Vergangenheit von *to be (was / were)* und dem Partizip der Vergangenheit des Hauptverbs gebildet.
- In einigen Passivsätzen erhalten Sie keine Auskunft über denjenigen, der die Handlung ausführte (A).
- In manchen Fällen erfahren Sie zwar auch, wer die Handlung ausführte, die Handlung aber wird zuerst genannt (B).
- Passivsätze können in allen Ihnen bekannten Zeiten gebildet werden (C).

A	Peter **is driven** to school every day. The children **were invited** to a party last weekend.
B	Their homework **is checked** by the teacher. The children **were entertained** by a clown.
C	We've got a new house. The kitchen **is being modernised**, the bathroom **has** just **been decorated** and the garden **is going to be landscaped** next month.

Rewrite these sentences in the passive. You needn't say who performs or performed the action.

1 People speak English in Malta. *English* ……………………………………………… .

2 They drank a lot of beer at the party. *A lot of beer* ……………………………………………… .

3 Someone left their keys on the table. *Someone's keys* ....

4 The bar serves drinks until midnight. *Drinks* .... S. 51

The passive – present and past

The passive – mixed tenses	39
The passive with two objects	39
The passive with *It is said, thought, expected,* etc.	40

Questions

A

- **Fragen** können mit einem Fragewort beginnen: *how, what, when, where, which, who, why.* (A)
- Sie können auch mit bestimmten Hilfsverben beginnen: *do, does, did, was, were,* etc. (B)
- Ein Modalverb kann ebenso das erste Wort einer Frage sein: *Can you ...?* (C)
- Fragen mit *to be* werden immer durch Wortumstellung gebildet. (D)

A	**When did you leave** school?	C	**Can you speak** Italian?
B	**Did you enjoy** your schooldays?	D	**Are you** good at languages?

Write the questions that give the information in bold.

1 Her name's **Brigitte.** ....

2 They arrived **on Monday.** ....

3 I'd like **the blue one,** please. ....

4 **Yes, I have.** I went to Paris last year. ....

5 **Yes, I can.** I learnt to swim when I was five. ....

6 **No, I don't.** I've always hated seafood. ....

7 He was angry **because I was late.** ....

8 **No, we didn't.** Yesterday we drank tea instead of coffee. .... S. 51

....

Questions

Questions with prepositions at the end	41
Subject / Object questions with *who*	41
Question tags	42

Reported (Indirect) speech – present to past

A

- Wenn das einleitende Verb (*say, tell*) in der Gegenwart steht, ändert sich die grammatische Verbzeit im untergeordneten Satz nicht: *"I can't hear it." – He says that he can't hear it.*
- Nur wenn das einleitende Verb in der Vergangenheit steht (*said, told*), ändert sich die grammatische Zeit des Verbs im untergeordneten Satz: *He said that he couldn't hear it.*

- Im Allgemeinen verschiebt sich die grammatische Zeit des Verbs im untergeordneten Satz um einen Schritt in die Vergangenheit zurück z.B. *can* ▸ *could, am / is* ▸ *was, are* ▸ *were, live* ▸ *lived*, etc.
- Sie können *that* verwenden oder auslassen: *He said (that) he couldn't hear it.*

"I **can ski** but I **can't skate.**"	She said (that) she **could ski** but she **couldn't skate.**
"I **am** late but I**'m not** worried."	He said (that) he **was** late but he **wasn't worried**.
"We **want** tea but we **don't want** any cake."	They said (that) they **wanted** tea but they **didn't want** any cake.

What did your boss say?

1 "I'm not happy with that work." He said that ....

2 "I can dictate it." He said that ....

3 "My secretary is ill." He said that ....

4 "I don't need the report." He said that ....

5 "I can't drive to the airport" He said that ....

S. 51 6 "I know her boss." He said that ....

Reported (Indirect) speech – present to past

Reported speech – mixed tenses	42
Reported questions	43
Reporting verbs	44

Modals of obligation and permission

A

- *Must, have to* und *can* sind **Modalverben**. Sie werden zusammen mit anderen Verben verwendet: *I must go now. Why do you have to leave now? I can't stay any longer.*
- *Must* und *can* haben in allen Personen identische Formen.

	Present and future	Past
positive	I **must leave** early.	I **had to leave** early.
negative	I **don't have to leave** yet. I **needn't leave** yet.	I **didn't have to leave** immediately.
question	**Do** you **have** to leave?	**Did** you **have** to leave?
positive	I **can stay** at home.	I **could stay** at home yesterday.
negative	I **can't stay** at home.	I **couldn't go** out yesterday.
question	**Can** you **stay** at home?	**Could** you **stay** at home yesterday?

- *Mustn't* wird verwendet, um auszudrücken, dass etwas nicht erlaubt oder nicht annehmbar ist: *Visitors mustn't park here. Must* = müssen, *mustn't* = nicht dürfen, *don't have to / needn't* = nicht müssen.
- Wenn wir *could* in der Vergangenheit im Sinne von *erlaubt sein* verwenden, können wir auch sagen: *I **was allowed to leave** when I had finished.*

Present or past? Complete these sentences.

1 I was so full. I (– can finish my dinner) ....

2 The car is clean. You (– have to clean it) ....

3 She missed her train. She (+ must wait for an hour) ....

4 We haven't seen that film. (? can join you) .... we ....

5 There was a queue. – (? have to wait long) .... you ....

6 Your exam is at 10. You (– must be late) .... S. 51

Modals of obligation and permission

Modals of ability	45
Modals of deduction	45
Modals of probability	46

First conditional

A

- ***If*-Sätze vom Typ 1** beschreiben Konsequenzen für den Fall, dass etwas in der Zukunft geschehen könnte (oder auch nicht).
- Sie werden im Hauptsatz mit der Zukunft mit *will* (*will* + Infinitiv) und im *if*-Satz mit der einfachen Gegenwart gebildet.

What **will you do if they offer** you that job?	**I'll accept** the job **if they offer** it to me.	**If I don't get** the job, **I won't be** terribly upset.
	I won't get a holiday this year **if I change** jobs. **If they don't offer** me this job, **I'll look** in the newspapers again.	

- **Rechtschreibung** Wenn der gesamte Satz mit *if* beginnt, müssen Sie vor dem Hauptsatz ein Komma setzen.

Cross out the wrong words.

1 If John *misses / will miss* his flight, he *is / 'll be* late for the meeting. 2 Susan *doesn't / won't* go out tonight if *she doesn't / won't* feel well. 3 Will they stay at the hotel if there *'s / will* be a room available? – Yes, they *do / will*. 4 If Bob *retires / will retire* early, he *has / will have* more time for his hobbies. 5 *Does / Will* the company expand if sales increase? – Yes, it *does / will*. 6 *Are they / Will they be* angry if we *don't / won't call?* – No, they *don't / won't*. S. 51

First conditional

First conditional with modals of probability	46

Second conditional

A

- ***If*-Sätze vom Typ 2** beschreiben eine Situation, die nicht existiert, die aber vorstellbar ist.
- Sie werden im Hauptsatz mit *would* + Infinitiv gebildet und im *if*-Satz mit der Vergangenheit.
- Die Verbformen sind in allen Personen identisch.
- Beim Verb *to be* ist es stilistisch besser, auch in der ersten und dritten Person *were* (anstelle von *was*) zu verwenden.

What **would you do** if **you saw** a robber outside your bank?	**I'd call** the police if **I had** my mobile phone with me.	If **I didn't have** my phone with me, **I probably wouldn't do** anything.
	I wouldn't try to stop the robber even if **he were** half my size. If **he didn't drive** away too fast, **I'd write** down his car number.	

- **Zeichensetzung** Wenn der gesamte Satz mit *If* beginnt, müssen Sie vor dem Hauptsatz ein Komma setzen.

Write sentences with *if* about these situations:

1 Susan doesn't have enough money, so she's not going on holiday this year.

If Susan .... , ...

2 I don't go for walks in the park because I haven't got a dog.

I .... if ....

3 I live in Glasgow because that's where my job is.

If my job .... , I ....

4 Kate drinks coffee every morning because it's free at her office.

S. 51 If the coffee .... , Kate ....

Second conditional — *Wish* and **second conditional** 47

Third conditional

A

- ***If*-Sätze vom Typ 3** werden verwendet, um über eine Situation in der Vergangenheit zu spekulieren. Man stellt sich vor, was passiert wäre oder hätte passieren können, wenn die Situation eine andere gewesen wäre
- Sie werden im Hauptsatz mit *would have* + dem Partizip der Vergangenheit (z.B. *done / been / gone etc.*) und im *if*-Satz mit der vollendeten Vergangenheit (z.B. *had done*) gebildet.

Would you have asked her out **if her boyfriend hadn't been** there?	**I would have phoned** her **if she had given** me her number.	**I wouldn't have met** her **if you hadn't introduced** us.
	I would have flirted with her **if her boyfriend hadn't been** there. **If she had been** alone, **she wouldn't have ignored** me.	

- **Rechtschreibung** Wenn der gesamte Satz mit *If* beginnt, müssen Sie vor dem Hauptsatz ein Komma setzen.

Write in the correct form of the words in brackets.

1 I didn't know she was in town. If I (+ know) ...., I (+ phone) .... her. **2** Our journey (+ be) .... better if there (– be) .... so much traffic. **3** (? go) .... you .... with them if they (+ ask) .... you? **4** If he (+ drive) .... more slowly, he (– get) .... a speeding ticket. **5** We (+ finish) .... the task earlier if we (+ begin) .... work sooner. **6** If she (– remind) .... him about his appointment, he (+ forget) ....

S. 52

Third conditional —— **Third conditional** with modals of probability 48

Wish

A

- ***I wish*** + **Vergangenheit** wird verwendet, um Unzufriedenheit mit einer Situation in der Gegenwart auszudrücken (A).
- ***I wish*** + **vollendete Vergangenheit** wird verwendet, um Bedauern über Vergangenes auszudrücken (B).
- ***I wish*** + **Person** + **would** + **Verb** kann verwendet werden, wenn wir wünschen, dass etwas geschehen möge, aber nicht sehr zuversichtlich sind (C).

A	Do you **wish you could speak** perfect English?	I **wish I lived** in an English-speaking country.	I **wish I didn't have to study** so hard.
B	Do you **wish you had worked** harder at school?	I **wish I had learnt** Spanish at school.	I **wish I hadn't learnt** Latin.
C	Do you **wish he would stop** smoking?	I **wish he would smoke** a pipe instead of cigars.	I **wish he wouldn't smoke** cigarettes.

Complete the sentences.

1 Kim can't play the guitar but she would really like to.

She wishes ....

2 Kate didn't go to the concert with Liz. Afterwards Liz said it was really good.

Kate wishes ....

3 You have to work in the office today. The weather outside is sunny and warm.

I wish ....

4 You didn't do the lottery last week but your usual numbers won the jackpot.

I wish ....

5 Your friend has ordered a salad with prawns by mistake. She doesn't like prawns.

She wishes ....

6 Your friend Don hates it when his girlfriend plays video games all day.

S. 52 He wishes ....

Wish

Wish and second conditional 47

Adjectives – comparative and superlative

A

- Adjektive dienen zur näheren Bestimmung von Substantiven.
- Sie sind in ihrer Form unveränderlich. *(a **young** girl, a **young** boy, some **young** children).*

Short adjectives	**Comparatives**	**Superlatives**
A is **long.**	B is **longer than** A, but **isn't as long as** C.	C is **the longest.**
Long adjectives	**Comparatives**	**Superlatives**
A is **exciting.**	B is **less exciting than** A, but **isn't as ... as** C.	C is **the least exciting.**

- **Unregelmäßige Formen** *good ▸ better than ▸ the best, bad ▸ worse than ▸ the worst*
- **Wichtig** Zweisilbige Adjektive auf *-y, -ow, -er, -le* verhalten sich wie kurze Adjektive: *sunny ▸ sunnier than ▸ the sunniest, clever ▸ cleverer than ▸ the cleverest*. Andere zweisilbige Adjektive verhalten sich wie lange Adjektive: *modern ▸ more modern ▸ the most modern*.
- **Rechtschreibung** Wenn im Auslaut ein Konsonant auf einen Vokal folgt, wird der Konsonant verdoppelt *(bigger)*. Wenn der letzte Buchstabe *-y* ist, wird *y* zu *i (heavier)*.

Write in the correct form of the adjectives in brackets.

1 In winter the days are (short) .... than in summer. **2** July is (hot) .... than May here. **3** This is the (crowded) .... disco in the city.

4 John isn't as (tall) .... as Jamie. **5** Yesterday was the (bad) .... day of my life. **6** Bruce is a (bad) .... golfer than Chris. **7** His car was (expensive) .... than mine. **8** That was the (tasty) .... meal I've ever eaten.

S. 52

Adjectives – comparative and superlative — **Adjectives** and adverbs 49

Adverbs – comparative

A

- Adverbien dienen zur näheren Bestimmung von Verben (Handlungen). Sie stehen im Satz nach dem Verb. *(He sings **beautifully**. She speaks **clearly**.)*
- Sie sind in ihrer Form unveränderlich. *(She eats **quickly**. He eats **quickly**. They eat **quickly**.)*
- Adverbien werden normalerweise gebildet, indem *-ly* an ein Adjektiv angehängt wird.
- **Unregelmäßige Formen** Die letzten vier Beispiele in der Tabelle sind unregelmäßig.

Adjective	Adverb	Adverb – comparative
She's a **slow** writer.	She writes **slowly**.	She writes **more slowly than** me.
They're **polite** children.	They speak **politely**.	They speak **more politely than** their friends.
He's a **careful** driver.	He drives **carefully**.	But he doesn't drive **as carefully as** me. He drives **less carefully than** me.
She's a **good** student.	She learns **well**.	She learns **better than** her sister.
He's a **bad** dancer.	He dances **badly**.	He dances **worse than** his girlfriend.
They're **hard** workers.	They work **hard**.	They work **harder than** me.
She's a **fast** runner.	She runs **fast**.	She runs **faster than** all the others.

- **Rechtschreibung** Bei Adjektiven auf *-y* wird *y* zu *i*, bevor *-ly* angehängt wird. *(happy ▸ happily)* Bei Adjektiven auf *-ic* wird *-ally* angehängt. *(enthusiastic ▸ enthusiastically)*

Write the correct words in the gaps.

1 We played (bad) ...., and the other team tried (hard) .... us. **2** Today it rained (heavy) .... yesterday. **3** She sang the song as (good) .... he did. **4** Kirk and Lisa smiled (happy) .... at their wedding. **5** I speak French less (fluent) .... them. **6** A mechanic can repair my car (fast) .... I can. **7** She can cook a lot (good) .... her husband.

S. 52

Adverbs – comparative — Adjectives and **adverbs** 49

A, an, some and any

A

- Aussagen über das Vorhandensein oder die Verfügbarkeit von etwas enthalten immer ***a***, ***an***, ***some*** oder ***any***.
- Damit Sie das richtige Wort wählen können, müssen Sie wissen, ob das Hauptwort **zählbar** oder **nicht zählbar** ist. Bedenken Sie, dass einige im Deutschen zählbare Wörter im Englischen nicht zählbar sind, z.B. *accommodation, advice, furniture, information, news.*
- Sie müssen außerdem wissen, ob es sich um einen Aussagesatz, einen verneinten Satz oder eine Frage handelt.

	question	**positive**	**Past**
countable	Is there **a** cinema or **an** opera house near your house?	There's **a** small cinema.	There isn't **an** opera house.
	Are there **any** secretaries, or managers in your class.	There are **some** secretaries.	There aren't **any** managers.
uncountable	Have you got **any** water, beer or wine at home?	I've got **some** beer.	I haven't got **any** wine.

- **Wichtig** *An* steht vor Hauptwörtern, die mit einem Selbstlaut beginnen: *an apple, an hour.*

Begin each question with *Is there a ..., Is there an ..., Is there any ...,* or *Are there any ...* and complete the answers.

1 .... news? – Yes, ... good news.
2 .... cigarettes in the packet? – No, ... left.
3 .... university near here? – No, but .... a high school. **4** .... advice you can give me? Yes, I can give you .... good advice. **5** .... lemon in the fruit bowl? No, but .... limes in the fridge.

S. 52

A, an, some and any — Quantifiers – *(a few, a great deal of,* etc.) 49

Defining relative clauses

A

- Sie können zwei Sätze durch ein Relativpronomen verbinden: *I saw a film yesterday. It was very good. = The film* ***which*** */* ***that*** *I saw yesterday was very good.*
- Bei Dingen können Sie als Relativpronomen *which* oder *that* verwenden (A).
- Bei Personen können Sie *who* oder *that* verwenden (B).
- Das Relativpronomen kann weggelassen werden, wenn der Relativsatz ein eigenes Subjekt hat (C). Aber wenn Sie das Relativpronomen verwenden, ist der Satz auf jeden Fall richtig.

A	The restaurant **which** was recommended to me was excellent. The book **that** won the prize was by an American.
B	The woman **who** lives upstairs is very quiet. The people **that** work with me are very friendly.
C	The holiday **(which)** *I* booked was a special offer. (*I* ist das Subjekt des Relativsatzes.) The people **(who)** *they* met at the party all came from Wales. (*they* ist das Subjekt des Relativsatzes.)

Write *who* or *which* in the six sentences which **must** have a relative pronoun. Leave the other gaps blank.

1 The man .... sold me my car was a criminal! **2** She shared a taxi with someone .... she'd met on the train. **3** I bought a fridge .... matches my kitchen. **4** The car .... won the race was driven by an Italian. **5** The new supermarket .... opened last week is a 24-hour one. **6** The teacher .... marked the tests was disappointed with his students. **7** I bought a souvenir for the neighbour .... looked after my cats. **8** I bought that book .... you told me about. **9** Have you got that pen .... I lent you last week?

S. 52

Defining relative clauses — Non-defining relative clauses 50

Stative (non-activity) verbs

B

- Die Verlaufsformen der Zeiten werden verwendet, um Handlungen zu beschreiben, die während eines bestimmten Zeitraums stattfinden: ***I'm waiting*** *for her.* Einige Verben werden selten in den Verlaufsformen verwendet, da sie Zustände und Gefühle beschreiben und keine Handlungen mit bewusstem Anfang und Ende: ***I am*** *angry because* ***I hate*** *waiting.*

Do you **like** detective stories? I **prefer** science fiction. I **don't need** anything to read.

Einige statische Verben: ***like, love, hate, need, want, prefer,***
believe, forget, know, realise, mean, seem, understand,
belong, contain, consist, cost

- Manche Verben können sowohl in der Verlaufsform als auch als statisches Verb verwendet werden: *Peter****'s looking*** *at his son's homework. He* ***doesn't look*** *very happy.*

Write the correct form of the verbs in brackets.

1 Sue (– like) .... Chinese food much but she (+ love) .... sushi. **2** Sorry, I (– understand) .... what you (+ try) .... to tell me. **3** This new brand of cola (– contain) .... sugar and it (+ cost) .... more. **4** She (+ have) .... a new car so she (+ have) .... driving lessons. **5** What (? think) .... you .... about? – I (– think) .... I (+ want) .... to tell you.

S. 52

Present simple and present progressive

B

- Einen Überblick über die Formen dieser Zeiten erhalten Sie auf Seite 7 (**Present simple**) und Seite 8 (**Present progressive**).
- Den Unterschied im Gebrauch der **einfachen Gegenwart** und der **Verlaufsform der Gegenwart** können Sie an diesem Satz gut erkennen:

She usually **goes** to work on foot, but today she**'s going** by bus.

Write the verbs in brackets in the **present simple** or the **present progressive**.

1 I (+ read) .... the newspaper every morning on the train. **2** What (? do) .... she .... ? – She (+ write) .... some e-mails. **3** Today we (+ drink) .... tea because there's no more coffee left. **4** Which languages (? speak) .... she .... ? – She (+ speak) .... English and Spanish. **5** Listen! They (+ play) .... my favourite song on the radio. – They (– play) .... it very often. **6** Susan normally (+ do) .... yoga on Tuesdays and Thursdays, but this week she (– go) .... at all.

S. 52

Present simple and present perfect simple

B

- Einen Überblick über die Formen dieser Zeiten erhalten Sie auf den Seiten 7 (**Present simple**) und 8 (**Present perfect simple**).
- Den Unterschied im Gebrauch der **einfachen Gegenwart** und der **einfachen Form vollendeten Gegenwart** können Sie an diesem Satz gut erkennen.

He **knows** my brother – they **have known** each other since their schooldays.

Write in the correct form of the verbs in brackets.

1 How many times (? read) .... she .... that book? – Three times, she (+ love) .... it. **2** (? miss) .... I .... the bus? – Yes, but a bus (+ come) .... every ten minutes. **3** (? be) .... you .... to the new boutique? – Yes, it (+ have) .... great clothes. **4** Now that Jane (+ stop) .... eating junk food she (+ feel) .... much healthier. **5** Bowling (+ sound) .... like fun. We (– do) .... that for a long time. **6** The Smiths (+ build) .... a new house but (– move in) .... yet.

S. 52

Present perfect simple and present perfect progressive

B

- Einen Überblick über die Formen dieser Zeiten erhalten Sie auf den Seiten 8 (**Present perfect simple**) und 9 (**Present perfect progressive**).
- Den Unterschied im Gebrauch der **einfachen Form** und der **Verlaufsform der vollendeten Gegenwart** können Sie an diesem Satz gut erkennen.

She **has known** him since her childhood and they **have been going** out together for ages.

- Die Verlaufsform wird nie mit statischen Verben gebraucht.
- Mit *how long* wird im Allgemeinen die Verlaufsform der vollendeten Gegenwart verwendet: *How long has he been smoking?*
- Mit *how much, how many, how often* oder *how far* wird im Allgemeinen die einfache Form der vollendeten Gegenwart verwendet: *How many cigarettes has he smoked?*

Write in the correct form of the words in brackets.

1 How long (? learn) .... Tim .... French? **2** The decorators (+ paint) .... the kitchen since lunchtime, but they (– finish) .... it yet. **3** I (+ stare) .... at my computer screen for hours. **4** He (+ look) .... for a new job for ages. How many interviews (? have) .... he ....? **5** It seems like we (+ drive) .... the whole day. How far (? come) .... we ....

S. 52

Present simple and present perfect progressive

B

- Einen Überblick über die Formen dieser Zeiten erhalten Sie auf Seite 7 (**Present simple**) und Seite 9 (**Present perfect progressive**).
- Den Unterschied im Gebrauch der **einfachen Gegenwart** und der **Verlaufsform der vollendeten Gegenwart** können Sie an diesem Satz gut erkennen:

She **works** for an airline, but she**'s been looking** for a new job since January.

1 Cross out the wrong word(s).

1 On Tuesdays we *have* / *have been having* dancing lessons. We *go* / *have been going* there for months. **2** He only *works* / *has been working* part-time. That's why he *doesn't work* / *hasn't been working* much lately. **3** How long *does Jim work* / *has Jim been working* at the bank? – Not long, but he really *likes* / *has been liking* his job there.

2 Write these sentences. ??? = *since* or *for*

1 usually | walk to work – but he | go by bus ??? his accident. He ……………………………………

……… .

2 live here ??? two years – and she | love her flat. She ……………………………………………

……… .

3 not like his new job – but he | only work there ??? last Monday. He ……………………………

S. 52

……… .

Past simple and present perfect simple

B

- Einen Überblick über die Formen dieser Zeiten erhalten Sie auf Seite 10 (**Past simple**) und Seite 8 (**Present perfect simple**).
- Den Unterschied im Gebrauch der **einfachen Vergangenheit** und der **einfachen Form der vollendeten Gegenwart** können Sie an diesen Sätzen gut erkennen:

I've been to New York twice – **I went** there last year and when **I was** ten years old.
Have you seen John yet? – Yes, **I saw** him about half an hour ago. Perhaps **he's** already **left**.

Write in the correct form of the verbs in brackets and complete the short answers.

1 A: I (+ be) ………………………… to lots of places – the one I (+ like) ……………… best (+ be) ……………… Africa.

2 B: Where exactly (? go) ……………… you …………… and what (? do) ……………… you ……………… there?

3 A: We mostly (+ travel) .... to West Africa and (+ meet) .... lots of fascinating people.

4 B: And (? take) .... you .... many photos when you (+ be) .... there?

5 A: Yes, we ...., but we (– put) .... them all into a photo album yet.

6 B: (? decide) .... you .... where your next holiday will be?

7 A: Yes, we .... John (+ want) .... always .... to see South America.

8 B: I (+ go) .... there two years ago and (+ hike) .... through the rain forest. But Ted (– come) .... with me – we (– be) .... together at that time.

S. 52

Used to

B

- Wir verwenden ***used to***, um über Dinge zu sprechen, die wir nur in der Vergangenheit getan haben: *She used to have ballet lessons.* (= Sie nimmt heute keine Ballettstunden mehr.)
- Nach *used to* folgt der Infinitiv: *used to see*, *used to go* usw.
- Die Frage und die Verneinung von *used to* werden in derselben Weise gebildet wie bei anderen Verben in Gegenwart und Vergangenheit.
- Die Verbformen sind in allen Personen identisch.

Did you use to walk to school when you were a child?	No, **I didn't use to walk** to school.	**I used to go** by bus.
Did she use to have violin lessons when she was young?	No, **she didn't use to have** violin lessons.	**She used to have** ballet lessons.

Complete these sentences using *used to* and a verb when necessary.

1 He's a vegetarian nowadays. – Yes, but when he was a child, ... meat.

2 He's a fitness fanatic now but .... 40 cigarettes a day.

3 No one knows their music any more but they .... famous.

4 She .... colour her hair but now that she does, it looks lovely.

5 Where .... you .... skiing when you were a child?

6 She .... next door to me but she moved last year.

7 I .... a school uniform.

8 .... you .... 'Children's Hour' on TV?

S. 52

Past simple and past progressive

B

- Einen Überblick über die Formen dieser Zeiten erhalten Sie auf Seite 10.
- Den Unterschied im Gebrauch der **einfachen Vergangenheit** und der **Verlaufsform der Vergangenheit** können Sie an diesen Sätzen gut erkennen:

They **were waiting** for the bus when it **began** to rain. When it **began** to rain, they **took** a taxi.
What **were** they **doing** when it began to rain? – They **were waiting** for a bus.
What **did** they **do** when it began to rain? – They **took** a taxi.

Write in the correct form of the verbs in brackets.

1 Jim (+ drive) .... on the motorway when his mobile phone (+ ring) .... **2** How fast (? drive) .... they .... when the police (+ stop) .... them? **3** After he (+ get) .... home, they (+ go) .... out for dinner. **4** I (+ write) .... an email when I (+ press) .... the wrong key and my screen (+ turn) .... black. **5** He (+ carry) .... a large box when he (+ trip) .... and (+ fall) .... **6** Vera (+ sit) .... in the café when a film star (+ sit) .... down near her.

S. 52

Past simple and past perfect simple

B

- Einen Überblick über die Formen dieser Zeiten erhalten Sie auf den Seiten 10 (**Past simple**) und 11 (**Past perfect simple**).
- Den Unterschied im Gebrauch der **einfachen Vergangenheit** und der **vollendeten Vergangenheit** können Sie an diesem Satz gut erkennen.

She **arrived** at the station but the train **had** already **left**.

Write the correct form of the verbs in brackets.

1 The boss (+ already go) .... home when I (+ leave) .... the office. **2** Jim (+ come) .... back from Paris on Sunday. He (+ be) .... there for two weeks. **3** Sorry I couldn't play tennis with you yesterday. I (+ just eat) .... lunch. **4** They (+ invite) .... me to dinner but I (+ already make) .... other plans.

S. 52

Past simple and past perfect progressive

B

- Einen Überblick über die Formen dieser Zeiten erhalten Sie auf Seite 10 (**Past simple**) und Seite 12 (**Past perfect progressive**).
- Den Unterschied im Gebrauch der **einfachen Vergangenheit** und der **Verlaufsform der vollendeten Vergangenheit** können Sie an diesen Sätzen gut erkennen:

How long **had** your mother **been working** at the hospital when she **left** her job?
She**'d been working** there for over thirty years when she **retired** last year.

Read the situations and complete the sentences.

1 Two football teams were playing in heavy rain. After sixty minutes the referee called off the match. – The players .... for over an hour when the referee .... the match.

2 Paul started learning French at the age of twenty. He first went to France ten years later. Paul .... when he first .... to France.

3 Kim came home from the party four hours late. Her parents were waiting for her in the sitting-room. – When Kim ...., her parents .... for her for four hours.

4 I know they travelled for a long time. They went to Thailand at some point, but I can't remember when. – Do you know how long they .... when they .... to Thailand?

S. 52

Past perfect simple and past perfect progressive

B

- Einen Überblick über die Formen dieser Zeiten erhalten Sie auf Seite 11 (**Past perfect simple**) und Seite 12 (**Past perfect progressive**).
- Mit *how long* verwenden wir normalerweise die **Verlaufsform der vollendeten Vergangenheit**; mit *how much, how many* oder *how often* verwenden wir normalerweise die **einfache Form der vollendeten Vergangenheit**.
- Denken Sie daran, dass einige Verben (*stative verbs*) wie *be, want, like, know, forget* usw. nicht in der Verlaufsform verwendet werden.
- Den Unterschied im Gebrauch der **einfachen Form** und der **Verlaufsform der vollendeten Vergangenheit** können Sie an diesem Satz gut erkennen:

They **had known** each other for two years and they**'d been living** together for ages when they got married.

Write in the correct form of the verb in brackets.

1 When the guests arrived, I (+ cook) .... for three hours. **2** When she got home, she didn't have her briefcase. She (+ leave) .... it at work. **3** The car door was unlocked. John (+ forget) .... to lock it when he parked. **4** She didn't want to see the film again because she (+ already see) .... it twice. **5** He sold the old house. It (+ belong) .... to his family for over 60 years. **6** When he answered the door, his hands were dirty. He (+ work) .... in the garden since lunchtime.

S. 52

Future simple and future progressive

B

- Einen Überblick über die Formen dieser Zeiten erhalten Sie auf Seite 12 (**Future simple**) und Seite 15 (**Future progressive**).
- Den Unterschied zwischen der **Zukunft mit *will*** und der **Verlaufsform der Zukunft** können Sie an diesem Satz gut erkennen.

She**'ll feel** happy when her presentation is over – she**'ll be doing** it at this time tomorrow.

Write the correct form of these verbs in the gaps.

call | have | pass | recognise | study | sail | wear | work

1 I can't go to the beach with you tomorrow because I .... for my exam. – Well I'm sure you .... it.

2 Where do you think you .... in five years' time? – Well, I expect I .... still .... the same job as now.

3 From the 8th to the 14th July, I .... on my yacht in Monaco. I .... you when I get back.

4 He .... definitely .... her, because he knows what she ....

S. 52

Future simple and future perfect

B

- Einen Überblick über die Formen dieser Zeiten erhalten Sie auf Seite 12 (**Future simple**) und Seite 16 (**Future perfect**).
- Den Unterschied zwischen der **Zukunft mit *will*** und der **vollendeten Zukunft** können Sie an diesem Satz gut erkennen.

She**'ll mail** the agenda to the participants tomorrow lunchtime – she**'ll have finished** it by then.

Write in the correct form of the verbs in brackets.

1 Carol is working on her essay. She (+ complete) .... it by tonight. **2** The tennis match (+ be) .... over in five minutes. **3** John's parents arrived on Monday. By Friday they (+ be) .... here for five days. **4** The manager (– be) .... here to greet you, she (+ leave) .... already .... **5** John (+ pack) .... the car by noon and then he (+ fill) .... the petrol tank.

S. 52

Future with *going to* and future with present progressive

B

- Einen Überblick über die Formen dieser Zeiten erhalten Sie auf den Seiten 13 (**Future with *going to***) und 15 (**Future with present progressive**).
- Den Unterschied im Gebrauch der **Zukunft mit *going to*** und der **Zukunft mit der Verlaufsform der Gegenwart** können Sie an diesem Satz gut erkennen.

I**'m going to relax** this evening because I**'m giving** an important presentation tomorrow.

- *Going to* kann sowohl für zukünftige Pläne als auch für Vereinbarungen gebraucht werden, die Verlaufsform der Gegenwart jedoch nur für zukünftige Vereinbarungen.
- Die Verlaufsform der Gegenwart wird häufig mit den Verben *go* und *come* verwendet: *She's going to (go to) work on Saturday.*

Write the verbs in brackets in the correct tense. Use the both *going to* future and the present progressive for future in each sentence.

1 He (+ have) .... an early night tonight because he (+ start) .... work at 6 a.m. tomorrow.

2 I (+ have) .... lunch with the boss on Friday. I think he (+ offer) .... me a promotion.

3 From next month, I (+ train) .... twice a week because I (+ run) .... in a marathon on September 1st.

4 Peter and I (+ play) .... golf tomorrow. I (+ wear) .... my new golfing trousers.

5 She (+ travel) .... to Nepal next month and she (+ climb) .... Mount Everest.

S. 52

Was going to

B

- ***Was / were going to*** wird verwendet, um Handlungen auszudrücken, die geplant oder erwartet wurden, aber nicht stattgefunden haben.

I **was going to give** her some chocolates but she said she was on a diet – so I didn't.
I **wasn't going to give** her money for her birthday but that was what she wanted – so I did.

Write the correct form of *going to* + one of these verbs in the gaps.

go | ring | drive | fly | play | stay | water

1 We .... into the city but our car broke down. **2** I .... you but my mobile's battery died. **3** Sarah .... to Paris but she decided to go by train. **4** They .... golf yesterday but the weather was bad. **5** I .... swimming but the water was too cold. **6** I .... the garden but then it started raining. **7** Paul .... in last night but then his friends rung him up and they arranged to meet in town.

S. 52

When, as soon as, etc.

B

- Wenn ein Nebensatz mit einem der folgenden Zeitausdrücke beginnt: ***when***, ***as soon as***, ***before***, ***after***, dann kann das Verb im Nebensatz nicht in einer Zeitform der Zukunft stehen. Möglich sind nur die einfache Form der Gegenwart oder der vollendeten Gegenwart.

I'll phone him	**when, as soon as, before, after**	the concert **ends.** the concert **has ended.**

Cross out the wrong words.

1 I *am writing / will write* to him when I *am / will be* on holiday. **2** Do *you see / Will you see* him before he *leaves / will leave* tomorrow? **3** He *probably goes / will probably go* home as soon as he *has received / will receive* the prize. **4** I don't think she *finishes / will finish* the report before she *leaves / will leave* the office. **5** After you *have drunk / will drink* your coffee, we *go / will* go shopping.

S. 52

Future progressive and future perfect

B

- Einen Überblick über die Formen dieser Zeiten erhalten Sie auf Seite 15 (**Future progressive**) und Seite 16 (**Future perfect**).
- Den Unterschied zwischen der **Verlaufsform der Zukunft** und der **vollendeten Zukunft** können Sie an diesem Satz gut erkennen.

She**'ll be working** on the details of her presentation until the end of the month but she**'ll have chosen** the theme by next week

Write in the correct form of the verbs in brackets and complete the short answers.

1 John works from 9 to 5. At 3 p.m. he (+ still work) .... At 6 p.m. he (– work) .... any longer, he (+ leave) .... work. **2** (? reach) .... the runners .... the finishing line in two hours? No, they .... They (+ still run) .... **3** This is a long queue! We (+ probably stand) .... here in an hour.

4 Company sales are so good, our boss predicts they (+ rise) .... by 50% by the end of May.

S. 53

Gerunds and infinitives: *stop, remember, try*

B

- Auf einige Verben wie ***stop***, ***remember*** und ***try*** können der Infinitiv oder das Gerund folgen – allerdings verändert sich dadurch die Bedeutung.

stop	He **stopped to have** a cigarette. Why **don't** you **stop smoking**?	**stop + infinitive** = aufhören, um etwas zu tun **stop + gerund** = aufhören, etwas zu tun
remember	**Did** he **remember to phone** her? I **remember telling** him to phone.	**remember + infinitive** = an etwas denken **remember + gerund** = sich erinnern
try	**Try to go** to sleep. **Try counting** sheep.	**try + infinitive** = versuchen **try + gerund** = ausprobieren

Write in the correct form of the verbs in brackets.

1 Did you remember (buy) .... eggs? – Sorry, I forgot to put them on the list.

2 We had a flat tyre. I tried (change) .... it myself but I couldn't do it.

3 The driver stopped the car (ask) .... for directions to the beach.

4 I had a great childhood. I remember (build) .... a tree-house with my dad.

5 Would you please stop (talk) .... I'm trying (work) ....

6 John has a bad habit. He never remembers (turn off) .... the light.

S. 53 7 This wine spot on the tablecloth won't go away. – Try (put) .... salt on it.

Have something done – mixed tenses

B

- Einen Überblick über die Satzstellung bei ***have something done*** erhalten Sie auf Seite 17.
- *Have something done* kann in allen Zeitformen verwendet werden.

Are you going to have your hair done **tomorrow**?	I had my hair cut **two weeks ago.**	But I haven't had it coloured **for over a month.**

Number the items in B and C to form logical sentences with *have something done*.

A	B	C
1 Our office has	☐ have their photos	☐ house cleaned?
2 Carol is	☐ do you have your	☐ designed by an architect.
3 How often	☐ had a new computer	☐ my boat repaired.
4 I don't have enough	☐ dentist's to have her	☐ system installed.
5 She had the dress	☐ money to have	☐ teeth cleaned.
6 Diane is going to the	☐ tailor-made for	☐ I was a student.
7 The children are going to	☐ fortune told since	☐ the winter ball.
8 I haven't had my	☐ having her new flat	☐ taken for the magazine.

S. 53

The passive – mixed tenses

B

- Einen Überblick darüber, wie das **Passiv** gebildet wird, erhalten Sie auf Seite 18.
- Das Passiv kann in allen Zeitformen verwendet werden.

Is the church **going to be renovated?**	The roof **was repaired** last year.	But the inside **hasn't been painted** yet.
Will the paintings **be restored?**	Some of them **are being restored** now.	But a few of them **can't be done** this year.

Rewrite these active sentences in the passive. It is not important to say who performed the action.

1 Someone has scratched my new car! My new car .... !
2 Security officers must check all luggage. All luggage ....
3 When do the dustmen collect the rubbish? When .... ?
4 They didn't invite us to the party. We ....
5 Workmen are repairing the roads today. The roads ....
6 They could deliver the couch today. The couch ....
7 The city's going to hold a meeting. A meeting .... S. 53

The passive with two objects

B

- Einen Überblick darüber, wie Sätze im **Passiv** gebildet werden, erhalten Sie auf Seite 18.
- Wenn Sie einen Aktivsatz in einen Passivsatz umwandeln, wird das Objekt des Aktivsatzes zum Subjekt des Passivsatzes (A).
- Wenn ein Aktivsatz zwei Objekte hat, können zwei unterschiedliche Passivsätze gebildet werden B).

	Active	Passive
A	Someone stole **my bike**.	**My bike** was stolen.
B	They presented **her** with **the trophy**.	**She** was presented with the trophy. **The trophy** was presented to her.

- Übliche Verben mit zwei Objekten: *ask, give, offer, pay, show, teach, tell.*

Rewrite these active sentences in the passive. Make two passive sentences each time. It is not important to say who performed the action.

1 The company gave Sue the job.

Sue .... The job ....

2 They offered the flat to her.

She .... The flat ....

3 They pay their workers £15 per hour.

Workers .... £15 per hour ....

4 They teach yoga to the children.

The children .... Yoga ....

5 The speaker told the audience a joke.

S. 53 The audience .... A joke ....

The passive with *It is said, thought, expected*, etc.

B

- Eine Form des **Passivs** wird verwendet, um allgemein verbreitete Überzeugungen zu formulieren (*Man sagt, dass …*)

Active	Passive
People say that boxing is dangerous.	**It is said that** boxing is dangerous. Boxing **is said to be** dangerous.

- Einige Verben, die häufig in dieser Weise verwendet werden sind: *believe, consider, expect, know, say, think.*

Rewrite these active sentences in the passive.

1 The police believe that the suspects are armed.

The suspects ....

2 Doctors consider garlic to be healthy.

Garlic ....

3 They expect that this will be the hottest summer on record.

It ....

4 People know that smoking causes cancer.

It ....

5 Everyone thinks that Julie and Bill are in love.

Julie and Bill ....

6 They say that John is a good guitar player.

It .... S. 53

Questions with prepositions at the end

B

- Einen Überblick darüber, wie **Fragen** gebildet werden, erhalten Sie auf Seite 19.
- Es gilt heute als eher veraltet, einen Satz mit einer Präposition zu beginnen. Normalerweise steht die Präposition am Ende des Satzes.

What are you looking **at**?	Who was he talking **to**?
Where do you come **from**?	Whose project is she interested **in**?
What did they speak **about**?	Which books is she keen **on**?

Write the words in the correct order and complete the question with one of the following prepositions: about | against | for | to | with

1 are kind what jacket of looking you ....

.... **2** my you which of did colleagues speak ....

.... **3** the did to go who disco you ....

.... **4** guess you thinking what can I'm

.... **5** many has how

he professional golfers played ....

.... S. 53

Subject / Object questions with *who*

B

- Einen Überblick darüber, wie **Fragen** gebildet werden, erhalten Sie auf Seite 19.
- Das Beispiel A in der Tabelle zeigt, wie eine Frage mit *who* nach dem Subjekt (Person oder Sache *vor* dem Verb) gebildet wird. *Who met him? = Wer traf ihn?*
- Das Beispiel B in der Tabelle zeigt, wie eine Frage mit *who* nach dem Objekt (Person oder Sache *nach* dem Verb) gebildet wird. *Who did he meet? = Wen traf er?*

A	**Peter** phoned her.	**Who phoned her?**	**Peter** did.
B	She loves **Paul**.	**Who does she love?**	**Paul**.

Write *who*-questions.

1 Susan waved to **someone.** – Who ....

2 **Someone** phoned Mary. – Who ....

3 She works for **someone.** – Who ....

4 I lent that DVD to **someone.** – Who ....

S. 53 5 **Someone** types her reports. – Who ....

Question tags

B

- **Frageanhängsel** können verwendet werden, um eine Bestätigung für etwas zu erhalten, das Sie für wahr halten: *I didn't give it to you, did I?*
- Sie können auch zur Eröffnung eines lockeren Gesprächs verwendet werden, wenn Sie lediglich eine Reaktion erhalten möchten: *You've met my sister, haven't you?*
- Bei einem bejahten Satz erscheint das Frageanhängsel in der verneinten Form (A). Bei einem verneinten Satz erscheint das Frageanhängsel in der bejahten Form (B).

A	It **is** cold in here, **isn't it**? We **attended** the same conference, **didn't we**?
B	You **can't speak** Chinese, **can you**? You **don't live** locally, **do you**?

- **Wichtig** Wenn Ihre Stimme am Ende des Frageanhängsels hoch geht, heißt das, dass Sie sich nicht sicher sind und um eine echte Antwort bitten. Wenn Ihre Stimme am Ende des Frageanhängsels hinunter geht, bedeutet das, dass Sie lediglich eine Bestätigung Ihrer Aussage möchten.

Complete these sentences with a question tag.

1 You weren't late, ...?

2 They aren't coming, ...?

S. 53 3 You have seen it, ...?

4 She really enjoyed it, ...?

5 They will stay, ...?

6 They love cats, ...?

Reported (Indirect) speech – mixed tenses

B

- Wenn das einleitende Verb in der Vergangenheit steht *(said, told)*, ändert sich die grammatische Zeit des Verbs im untergeordneten Satz: *"I can't hear it." – He said that he couldn't hear it.*
- Im Allgemeinen verschiebt sich die grammatische Zeit des Verbs im untergeordneten Satz um einen Schritt in die Vergangenheit zurück. *Is* wird zu *was*. Achtung: *Will* wird zu *would*.
- Sie können *that* auslassen: *He said (that) he couldn't hear it.*

"I **am** ill."	She said (that) she **was** ill.
"He **is working**."	She told me (that) he **was working**.
"We **are** going to see her."	They said (that) they **were going to** see her.
"I **have visited** her."	She said (that) she **had visited** her.
"I **have been waiting** for ages."	She told me (that) she **had been waiting** for ages.
"I **want** to see you"	She said (that) she **wanted** to see me.
"We **drove** to her house."	They said (that) they **had driven** to her house.
"We **can't stay** long."	They said (that) they **couldn't stay** long.
"I **will be** quiet."	He said (that) he **would be** quiet.

John is checking the messages on his answerphone. What did the people say?

1 "I have reserved a table." His wife said that she ....

2 "I need to talk to you." His mother told him she ....

3 "You can have a week off." His boss said that he ....

4 "Your lunch is ready." The waiter said that his lunch ....

5 "We're coming over." His friends said that they ....

6 "I'll ring you later." George told me that ....

7 "I've been calling all day." His mother said she .... S. 53

Reported questions

B

- Fragen können mit einem Fragewort (*How, What, Where, Why,* etc.) oder mit einem Hilfsverb (*Did, Are, Can, Does, Will,* etc.) gebildet werden. Wenn eine Frage mit einem Hilfsverb in der indirekten Rede wiedergegeben wird, müssen *if* oder *whether* verwendet werden.
- Wenn das einleitende Verb in der Vergangenheit steht (*asked*), verschiebt sich das Verb in der Frage um einen Schritt in die Vergangenheit zurück: *Is* wird zu *was*. Achtung: *Will* wird zu *would*.

	Reporting verb in the past	Question word / if / whether	Subject	Verb in the past
"Where is it?"	He **asked** me	**where**	**it**	**was.**
"Will you do it?"	He **asked** me	**if / whether**	**I**	**would do it.**

A man is talking about a job interview he had. Look at the interviewer's questions and complete the reported questions below.

1 "Where have you worked so far?"
2 "Why did you leave your last job?"
3 "Are you looking for full-time work?"
4 "Do you mind working overtime?"
5 "Can you work under pressure?"
6 "How many languages do you speak?"
7 "What hobbies do you have?"
8 "When can you start?"

1 She asked me ....
2 She asked me ....
3 She asked me ....
4 She asked me ....
5 She asked me ....
6 She asked me ....
7 She asked me ....
S. 53 8 She asked me ....

Reporting verbs

B

- Es gibt viele Alternativen zu *say* als einleitendem Verb in der indirekten Rede.
- Sehen Sie sich genau an, was auf diese Verben im Satz folgt.

He **explained, repeated, replied**	that he **liked** it.	(+ Zeitverschiebung)
He **told, advised, asked, reminded**	**me** what to do.	(+ Person)
He **suggested, mentioned, apologised for**	**doing** it.	(+ Gerund)
He **agreed, refused, promised**	**to do** it.	(+ Infinitiv)

Cross out the wrong words:

A couple was stopped by a police officer who (**1**) *explained / advised* that the driver had been going too fast. The driver (**2**) *asked / replied* that it was an emergency as his wife was having a baby. The officer suggested (**3**) *taking / to take* a taxi instead. The husband had wanted to call a taxi, but his wife (**4**) *mentioned / refused* to go in a strange car. Suddenly, his wife looked panicky and (**5**) *reminded / repeated* him to hurry. The husband (**6**) *apologised for / refused* driving too fast and (**7**) *asked / suggested* the officer to help him. He (**8**) *agreed / told* and promised (**9**) *escorting / to escort* them to hospital. The woman (**10**) *repeated / told* that they had to hurry.

S. 53

Modals of ability

B

- *Can* und *could* sind **Modalverben**, mit deren Hilfe die Fähigkeit einer Person etwas zu tun ausgedrückt werden kann: Sie werden zusammen mit anderen Verben verwendet: *Can he play tennis? He could play tennis when he was six.*
- *Could* wird in der Vergangenheit verwendet, um allgemeine Fähigkeit auszudrücken: *He could play tennis well when he was young.* Wenn Sie sagen möchten, dass jemand fähig war, etwas in einer bestimmten Situation zu tun, verwenden Sie *able to: He was able to win the school trophy three times.*
- *Can* und *could* haben in allen Personen identische Formen.

Past	Present	Future
He **could play** the violin when he was ten. He **was able to get** a place at the conservatory.	He **can play** the piano well.	He**'ll be able to get** a job in an orchestra.

Cross out the incorrect word or words in each sentence.

1 He *can / could* play the piano when he was young. **2** He *could / will be able to* repair his own car when he finishes the mechanics course. **3** *Can you / Were you able to* get tickets for the opera last month? **4** *Can / Could* cats see in the dark? **5** She *wasn't able / won't be able* to find a partner on the Internet although she tried lots of times. **6** He *could / was able to* get the job because he spoke English well.

S. 53

Modals of deduction

B

- *Must, can* und *could,* sind **Modalverben**, mit deren Hilfe logische Schlussfolgerungen ausgedrückt werden. Sie werden zusammen mit anderen Verben verwendet: *Who can that be? It can't be the postman. It must be the electrician.*
- *Must, can,* und *could* haben in allen Personen identische Formen.

Present and future	Past
That **must be** a disco I can hear.	That **must have been** a disco I could hear.
It **could be** a party.	It **could have been** a party.
It **can't be** her birthday party.	It **couldn't have been** her birthday party.

Write in the correct form of the verbs in brackets.

1 He failed the exam so he (could / study) .... very hard.

2 Her birthday's next month. It (can / be) .... her birthday today.

3 The grass is wet. It (must / rain) .... in the night.

4 There's no message but he (could / phone) .... while I was out.

5 She looks so much like Peter. She (must / be) .... his sister.

S. 53 6 She's so young that she (can / be) .... his mother.

Modals of probability

B

- *Could, may* und *might* sind **Modalverben**, mit deren Hilfe Wahrscheinlichkeit oder Möglichkeit ausgedrückt werden können. Sie werden zusammen mit anderen Verben verwendet: *Could he be there already? He may arrive tomorrow. He might not come at all.*
- *Could, may* und *might* haben in allen Personen identische Formen.

Present and future	Past
He **could be** late.	He **could have been** late.
He **may come** by car.	He **may have come** by car.
He **might miss** the train.	He **might have missed** the train.

Cross out the **one** incorrect phrase in each sentence.

1 Who's that at the door? – It *may have been / could be / might be* the postman. 2 You'll probably see him. He *may arrive / might have arrived / might arrive* tomorrow. 3 He's late – he *may have had / might have had / could have* a crash. 4 It *could rain / might not rain / couldn't have rained* tomorrow. 5 He *might not have looked / might not look / could have looked* at his e-mails yesterday.

S. 53

First conditional with modals of probability

B

- Überblicke über diese Strukturen erhalten Sie auf Seite 21 (**First conditional**) und auf dieser Seite (**Modals of probability**).
- Im Hauptsatz eines *If*-Satzes vom Typ 1 kann *will* durch eine Hilfsverb der Wahrscheinlichkeit ersetzt werden.

If that party wins the election,	he will become the president.	✓✓✓
	he **could** become the president.	✓✓
	he **might** become the president.	✓
	he won't become the president.	✗

Write first conditional sentences with the words given. Use the structures in the box above.

1 they – invite me / I – ✓✓✓ go to the party.

....

2 He – ✓ catch the train / it – be a few minutes late.

....

3 We – ✗ have lunch / it be too expensive.

....

4 he – ✓ stay with Bill / he go to Berlin

....

5 I – ✓✓ visit you in Paris / you not mind.

.... S. 53

Wish and second conditional

B

- Überblicke über diese Sturkturen erhalten Sie auf Seite 23 (***Wish***) und auf Seite 22 (**Second conditional**)
- Beide Strukturen werden verwendet, um vorstellbare Situationen in der Gegenwart auszudrücken.

I wish I had enough money to buy a new car – but I don't. **If I had** enough money, **I would buy** a new car.

For each situation write the first sentence with *I wish* ... and the second sentence in the second conditional.

1 I'm unhappy because it's cold outside. I wish it (– be) .... so cold .

If it (– be) .... so cold, I (+ go) .... cycling.

2 I don't have any suntan lotion with me. I wish I (+ have) .... some.

I (+ lie) .... in the sun all day if I (+ have) .... some suntan lotion.

3 My French isn't very good. I wish (+ can speak) .... it better.

If I (+ can speak) .... it better, I (+ work) .... in Paris this summer.

4 Mark isn't very muscular. He wishes (+ be) .... more muscular. He thinks if

he (+ have) .... more muscles, he (+ impress) .... the girls.

5 Sheila can't sing very well. She wishes (+ can sing) .... well . If she

S. 53

(+ can sing) .... better, she (+ enter) .... a contest.

Third conditional with modals of probability

B

- Überblicke über diese Strukturen erhalten Sie auf Seite 22 (**Third conditional**) und Seite 46 (**Modals of probability**).
- Im Hauptsatz eines *if*-Satzes vom Typ 3 kann *would* ersetzt werden durch ein Modalverb der Wahrscheinlichkeit in der Vergangenheit.

If that party had won the election,	he would have become the president. he **could have** become the president. he **might have** become the president. he wouldn't have become the president.

Write in the correct form of the verbs in brackets and match the sentence halves together.

1 If he hadn't missed his bus,	☐ she (could / buy) .... that dress.
2 If she had applied for the job,	☐ they (could / win) .... the match.
3 If the team had played better,	☐ I (might / say) .... yes.
4 If you had asked me for help earlier,	☐ she (might / get) .... it.
5 If I'd had a pen and paper,	☐ I (would / write) .... you a note.
6 If she hadn't spent all her money,	☐ he (would / arrive) .... on time.

S. 53

Adjectives and adverbs

B

- Überblicke über diese Bereiche erhalten Sie auf Seite 24 (**Adjectives**) und Seite 25 (**Adverbs**).
- Den Unterschied zwischen **Adjektiven** und **Adverbien** können Sie an diesem Satz gut erkennen.

Our neighbours are very **loud** – they play **loud** music and they speak **loudly**, too.

Write in the correct form of the word in brackets.

1 We had a really (enjoy) .... holiday in Spain last month. **2** Our hotel was (luxury) .... and the staff were (friend) .... and most of them could speak English (fluent) .... **3** I tried to speak a bit of Spanish but I don't speak it very (good) .... **4** The weather was (fine) ...., except for one day when it rained (heavy) .... **5** Time passed so (fast) .... and the holiday seemed really (short) .... **6** It's strange that time always passes (quick) .... when you're on holiday and so (slow) .... when you're at work!

S. 53

Quantifiers (*a few, a great deal of*, etc.)

B

- Einen Überblick über **zählbare** und **nicht zählbare Wörter** erhalten Sie auf Seite 26 (***A***, ***an***, ***some*** and ***any***).
- Wenn wir über Mengen sprechen, wird das zu verwendende Wort oft dadurch bestimmt, ob das Hauptwort zählbar oder nicht zählbar ist.

Countable	**Uncountable**	**Countable + uncountable**
not many	not much	
a few / very few	a little / very little	hardly any
a couple (of)	a bit (of)	some
a large number (of)	a large amount (of)	plenty (of)
a great many	a great deal (of)	a lot (of) / lots (of)

Cross out the incorrect words in each sentence.

1 There's *hardly any / very few* bread left. **2** *A lot of / a great deal of* footballers kick with their left foot. **3** The police found *very few / a great deal of* clues at the crime scene. **4** We have *very little / a few* time to finish the project. **5** *A great many / a large amount of* fans went to see their favourite band. **6** I still have work to do so I'm going to stay *a couple of / not much* hours longer. **7** Your mother always has *a bit of / a large number of* good advice. **8** They gave us *a few / plenty of* information.

S. 53

Non-defining relative clauses

B

- Nicht bestimmende Relativsätze sind Sätze mit „zusätzlicher Information". Wir können Informationen zum Satz hinzufügen, indem wir einen Relativsatz einfügen: *My holiday started in June.* ▸ *My holiday, **which I spent in Greece,** started in June.*
- Wie in bestimmenden Relativsätzen verwenden wir *which* für Dinge, *who* für Menschen, *where* für Orte und *whose* für den Besitzfall.

The hotel,	**which** was near the sea,	was expensive.
The manager,	**who** reserved our rooms,	was from Spain.
The island,	**where** I spent my last week,	was fantastic.
The manager,	**whose** brother is a cook,	recommended the restaurant.

- **Zeichensetzung** Wir setzen ein Komma vor und nach dem nicht bestimmenden Relativsatz – außer, wenn der Relativsatz am Ende des gesamten Satzes steht. *I stayed in the Luxus hotel, **which** my sister recommended.*
- **Wichtig** In nicht bestimmenden Relativsätzen können *who* oder *which* weder durch *that* ersetzt noch ausgelassen werden.

Put the information in brackets into the main sentence. Don't forget the commas.

1 The new bridge will be open soon. (It was expensive to build.)

The new bridge ....

....

2 John went to the Niagara Falls. (He spent his holiday in Canada.)

John ....

....

3 The Smiths live in the Bahamas. (Their children are all grown-up.)

The Smiths ....

....

4 Manchester is his favourite city. (He lived there for three years.)

Manchester ....

S. 53 ....

Key / Lösungsschlüssel

Seite 7 – **Present simple**: 1 1 take / arrives 2 open 3 like 4 does / start 5 finishes 6 doesn't 7 Do / don't
2 1 eats 2 washes 3 Does / get up 4 doesn't like 5 do 6 don't know 7 tries 8 do / watch 9 tries / comes
Seite 8 – **Present progressive**: 1 I am not learning French. / Are you learning French? / They're learning French. 2 They aren't working today. / He isn't working today. / Is he working today?
Seite 8 – **Present perfect simple**: 1 Has / opened yet / hasn't / have already finished 2 Has / happened 3 Have / had / yet / have just ordered 4 Have / ever tried / have
Seite 9 – **Present perfect progressive**: 1 has been looking / for 2 have / been living 3 haven't been waiting 4 has been working 5 has been learning / since 6 hasn't been getting
Seite 10 – **Past simple**: 1 did / do / visited 2 Were / stayed 3 Did / go / flew 4 Did / see / didn't / went 5 was / ate / drank
Seite 10 – **Past progressive**: 1 was travelling / wasn't working 2 Was / jogging / was raining 3 were / partying 4 was riding / wasn't wearing 5 Were / lying / was writing
Seite 11 – **Past perfect simple**: 1 had / finished 2 hadn't eaten 3 Had / been / hadn't 4 had changed 5 had put / hadn't 6 hadn't broken
Seite 12 – **Past perfect progressive**: 1 had been sitting 2 hadn't been driving 3 Had / been missing / hadn't 4 Had / been working / had 5 had been trying 6 had / been writing 7 Had / been negotiating / had
Seite 12 – **Future simple**: 1 'll bring 2 'll finish / will 3 'll make 4 Will / be / won't / 'll phone 5 'll carry 6 'll cost
Seite 13 – **Future with going to**: 1 are / going to get married 2 is / going to wear 3 aren't going to get married 4 is going to take 5 are going to 6 am going to throw
Seite 14 – **Future with present simple**: 1 takes off / lands 2 finishes 3 closes 4 changes 5 go 6 run
Seite 15 – **Future with present progressive**: 1 is playing 2 are having / Are / coming / am 3 are / leaving 4 Are / working / am / isn't 5 Are / doing / am / am going 6 Are / flying / aren't / are driving
Seite 15 – **Future progressive**: 1 will be visiting / won't be arriving / will / be staying 2 will / be sleeping / won't be getting up / will / be dreaming 3 will / be doing / will be showing / won't be having
Seite 16 – **Future perfect**: 1 will have had 2 Will / have finished 3 won't have found 4 will have swum 5 won't have spent 6 Will / have given
Seite 17 – **Gerunds and infinitives**: 1 reserving 2 to drive 3 going 4 looking after 5 making 6 to fly 7 helping 8 to be
Seite 17 – ***Have something done* – present and past**: 1 I always have my groceries delivered. 2 She had her house painted last year. 3 He usually has his washing done for him. 4 We had a garage built last month. 5 They have their grass cut regularly. 6 We had all our bedrooms decorated last year.
Seite 18 – **The passive – present and past**: 1 is spoken in Malta. 2 was drunk at the party. 3 were left on the table. 4 are served until midnight.
Seite 19 – **Questions**: 1 What's her name? 2 When did they arrive? 3 Which one would you like? 4 Have you ever been to Paris? 5 Can you swim? 6 Do you like seafood? 7 Why was he angry? 8 Did you drink any coffee yesterday?
Seite 19 – **Reported (Indirect) speech – present to past**: 1 he wasn't happy with that work. 2 he could dictate it. 3 his secretary was ill. 4 didn't need the report. 5 he couldn't drive to the airport. 6 he knew her boss.
Seite 20 – **Modals of obligation and permission**: 1 couldn't finish my dinner. 2 don't have to clean it. 3 had to wait for an hour. 4 Can / join you? 5 Did / have to wait long? 6 mustn't be late.
Seite 21 – **First conditional**: 1 misses / 'll be late 2 won't / doesn't 3 's / will 4 retires / will have 5 Will / will 6 Will they / don't / won't
Seite 22 – **Second conditional**: 1 had enough money, she would go on holiday. 2 would go for walks in the park/ I had a dog. 3 wasn't/weren't in Glasgow / wouldn't live there. 4 wasn't/weren't free / wouldn't drink it.

Seite 22 – **Third conditional**: 1 had known / would have phoned 2 would have been / hadn't been 3 Would / have gone / had asked 4 had driven / wouldn't have got 5 would have finished / had begun 6 hadn't reminded / would have forgotten

Seite 23 – ***Wish***: 1 she could play the guitar. 2 she had gone to the concert. 3 I could go outside. / I didn't have to work. 4 I had done the lottery. 5 she hadn't ordered it. 6 she wouldn't play video games all day.

Seite 24 – **Adjectives – comparative and superlative**: 1 shorter 2 hotter 3 most crowded 4 tall 5 worst 6 worse 7 more expensive 8 tastiest

Seite 25 – **Adverbs – comparative**: 1 badly / harder than 2 more heavily than 3 well as 4 happily 5 fluently than 6 faster than 7 better than

Seite 26 – ***A, an, some* and *any***: 1 Is there any / there's some 2 Are there any / there aren't any 3 Is there a / there's 4 Is there any / some 5 Is there a / there are some

Seite 26 – **Defining relative clauses**: 1 who 2 – 3 which *bzw.* that 4 which *bzw.* that 5 which *bzw.* that 6 who 7 who 8 – 9 –

Seite 27 – **Stative (non-activity) verbs**: 1 doesn't like / loves 2 don't understand / are trying 3 doesn't contain / costs 4 has / is having 5 are / thinking / don't think / want

Seite 28 – **Present simple and present progressive**: 1 read 2 is / doing / is writing 3 are drinking 4 does / speak / speaks 5 are playing / don't play 6 does / isn't going

Seite 28 – **Present simple and present perfect simple**: 1 has / read / loves 2 Have / missed / comes 3 Have / been / has 4 has stopped / feels 5 sounds / haven't done 6 have built / haven't moved in

Seite 29 – **Present perfect simple and present perfect progressive**: 1 has / been learning 2 have been painting / haven't finished 3 have been staring 4 has been looking / has / had 5 have been driving / have / come?

Seite 30 – **Present simple and present perfect progressive**: 1 1 have / have been going 2 works / hasn't been working 3 has Jim been working / likes 2 1 usually walks to work but he has been going by bus since his accident. 2 has been living here for two years and she loves her flat. 3 doesn't like his new job but he has only been working there since last Monday.

Seite 30 – **Past simple and present perfect simple**: 1 have been / liked / was 2 did / go / did / do 3 travelled / met 4 did / take / were 5 did / haven't put 6 Have / decided 7 have / has / wanted 8 went / hiked / didn't come / weren't

Seite 31 – ***Used to***: 1 he used to eat 2 he used to smoke 3 used to be 4 didn't use to 5 did / use to go 6 used to live 7 used to wear 8 Did / use to watch

Seite 32 – **Past simple and past progressive**: 1 was driving / rang 2 were /driving / stopped 3 got / went 4 was writing / pressed / turned 5 was carrying / tripped / fell 6 was sitting / sat

Seite 32 – **Past simple and past prefect simple** : 1 had already gone / left 2 came / had been 3 had just eaten 4 invited / had already made

Seite 33 – **Past simple and past perfect progressive**: 1 had been playing / called off 2 had been learning French for ten years / went 3 came home / had been waiting 4 had been travelling for / went

Seite 33 – **Past perfect simple and past perfect progressive**: 1 had been cooking 2 had left 3 had forgotten 4 had already seen 5 had belonged 6 had been working

Seite 34 – **Future simple and future progressive**: 1 will be studying / will pass 2 will be working / will / have 3 will be sailing / will call 4 will/ recognise / will be wearing

Seite 35 – **Future simple and future perfect**: 1 will have completed 2 will be 3 will have been 4 won't be / will have / left 5 will have packed / will fill

Seite 35 – **Future with *going to* and future with present progressive**: 1 is going to have / starting 2 am having / is going to offer 3 am going to train / am running 4 are playing / am going to wear 5 is travelling / is going to climb

Seite 36 – ***Was going to***: 1 were going to drive 2 was going to ring 3 was going to fly 4 were going to play 5 was going to go 6 was going to water 7 was going to stay

Seite 37 – ***When, as soon as,* etc**: 1 will write / am 2 Will you see / leaves 3 will probably go / has received 4 will finish / leaves 5 have drunk / will go

Seite 37 – **Future progressive and future perfect**: 1 will still be working / won't be working / will have left 2 Will / have reached / won't / will still be running 3 will probably be standing 4 will have risen
Seite 38 – **Gerunds and Infinitives: *stop, remember, try*** : 1 to buy 2 to change 3 to ask 4 building 5 talking / to work 6 to turn off 7 putting
Seite 38 – ***Have something done* (mixed tenses)**: 1 Our office has had a new computer system installed. 2 Carol is having her new flat designed by an architect. 3 How often do you have your house cleaned? 4 I don't have enough money to have my boat repaired. 5 She had the dress tailor-made for the winter ball. 6 Diane is going to the dentist's to have her teeth cleaned. 7 The children are going to have their photos taken for the magazine. 8 I haven't had my fortune told since I was a student.
Seite 39 – **The passive – mixed tenses**: 1 has been scratched 2 must be checked 3 is the rubbish collected 4 weren't invited to the party 5 are being repaired today 6 could be delivered today 7 is going to be held
Seite 39 – **The passive with two objects**: 1 was given the job. / was given to Sue. 2 was offered the flat. / was offered to her. 3 are paid £15 per hour. / is paid to their workers. 4 are taught yoga. / is taught to the children. 5 were told a joke. / was told to the audience.
Seite 40 – **The passive with *It is said, thought, expected,* etc.**: 1 are believed to be armed. 2 is considered to be healthy. 3 is expected to be the hottest summer on record. 4 is known that cancer is caused by smoking. 5 are thought to be in love. 6 is said that John is a good guitar player.
Seite 41 – **Questions with prepositions at the end**: 1 What kind of jacket are you looking for? 2 Which of my colleagues did you speak to? 3 Who did you go to the disco with? 4 Can you guess what I'm thinking about? 5 How many professional golf players has he played against?
Seite 41 – **Subject/ Object questions with *who***: 1 Who did Susan wave to? 2 Who phoned Mary? 3 Who does she work for? 4 Who did you lend that DVD to? 5 Who types her reports?
Seite 42 – **Question tags**: 1 were you 2 are they 3 haven't you 4 didn't she 5 won't they 6 don't they
Seite 42 – **Reported (Indirect) speech – mixed tenses**: 1 had reserved a table. 2 needed to talk to him. 3 could have a week off. 4 was ready. 5 were coming over. 6 he would ring me later. 7 had been calling all day.
Seite 43 – **Reported questions**: 1 where I had worked so far. 2 why I had left my last job. 3 if I was looking for full-time work. 4 if I minded working overtime. 5 if I could work under pressure. 6 how many languages I spoke. 7 what hobbies I had 8 when I could start.
Seite 44 – **Reporting verbs**: 1 explained 2 replied 3 taking 4 refused 5 reminded 6 apologised for 7 asked 8 agreed 9 to escort 10 repeated
Seite 45 – **Modals of ability**: 1 could 2 will be able to 3 Were you able to 4 Can 5 wasn't able 6 was able to
Seite 45 – **Modals of deduction**: 1 couldn't have studied 2 can't be 3 must have rained 4 could have phoned 5 must be 6 can't be
Seite 46 – **Modals of probability**: 1 could be / might be 2 may arrive / might arrive 3 may have had / might have had 4 could rain / might not rain 5 might not have looked / could have looked
Seite 46 – **First conditional with modals of probability**: 1 If they invite me, I'll go to the party. 2 He might catch the train if it's a few minutes late. 3 We won't have lunch if it's too expensive. 4 He might stay with Bill if he goes to Berlin. 5 I could visit you in Paris if you don't mind.
Seite 47 – ***Wish* and second conditional**: 1 wasn't/weren't / wasn't/weren't / would go 2 had / would lie / had 3 could speak / could speak / would work 4 he was/were / had / would impress 5 could sing / could sing / would enter
Seite 48 – **Third conditional with modals of probability**: 1 he would have arrived on time. 2 she might have got it. 3 they could have won the match. 4 I might have said yes. 5 I would have written you a note. 6 she could have brought that dress.
Seite 49 – **Adjectives and adverbs**: 1 enjoyable 2 luxurious / friendly / fluently 3 well 4 fine / heavily 5 fast / short 6 quickly / slowly
Seite 49 – **Quantifiers (*a few, a great deal of* etc.)**: 1 hardly any 2 A lot of 3 very few 4 very little 5 A great many 6 a couple of 7 a bit of 8 plenty of
Seite 50 – **Non-defining relative clauses**: 1 The new bridge, which was expensive to build, will be open soon. 2 John, who spent his holiday in Canada, went to the Niagara Falls. 3 The Smiths, whose children are all grown up, live in the Bahamas. 4 Manchester, where he lived for three years, is his favourite city.

Grammar terminology / Grammatikbezeichnungen

Englisch	Deutsch / Lateinisch
Adjective	Eigenschaftswort / Adjektiv
Adverb	Umstandswort / Adverb
Comparative	1. Steigerungsstufe / Komparativ
Countables	Zählbare Wörter
Defining relative clause	Bestimmender Relativsatz
First Conditional	*If*-Satz vom Typ 1
Future perfect	Vollendete Zukunft / Futur II
Future progressive	Verlaufsform der Zukunft
Future simple	Einfache Zukunft
Future with *going to*	Zukunft mit *going to*
Future with present simple	Zukunft mit der einfachen Gegenwart
Gerund	*ing*-Form / Gerundium
Imperative	Befehlsform / Imperativ
Indirect speech	Indirekte Rede
Infinitive	Infinitiv / Grundform
Modals of ability	Modalverben der Fähigkeit
Modals of deduction	Modalverben der Schlussfolgerung
Modals of obligation	Modalverben der Verpflichtung
Modals of permission	Modalverben der Erlaubnis
Modals of probability	Modalverben der Wahrscheinlichkeit
Non-defining relative clause	Nicht bestimmender Relativsatz
Object	Satzergänzung / Objekt
Passive	Passiv / Leideform
Past perfect progressive	Verlaufsform der vollendeten Vergangenheit
Past perfect simple	Einfache Form der vollendeten Vergangenheit
Past participle	Partizip der Vergangenheit / Partizip Perfekt
Past progressive	Verlaufsform der Vergangenheit
Past simple	Einfache Vergangenheit
Personal pronoun	Persönliches Fürwort / Personalpronomen
Preposition	Verhältniswort / Präposition
Present perfect progressive	Verlaufsform der vollendeten Gegenwart
Present perfect simple	Einfache Form der vollendeten Gegenwart
Present progressive	Verlaufsform der Gegenwart
Present simple	Einfache Gegenwart
Pronoun	Fürwort / Pronomen
Quantifier	Mengenwort
Question tag	Frageanhängsel
Question word	Fragewort / Interrogativpronomen
Relative clause	Relativsatz

Englisch	Deutsch / Lateinisch
Relative pronoun	Bezügliches Fürwort / Relativpronomen
Reported question	Indirekte Frage
Reported speech	Indirekte Rede
Second conditional	*If*-Satz vom Typ 2
Short answers	Kurzantworten
Stative verb	Statisches Verb / Verb ohne Verlaufsform
Subject	Satzgegenstand / Subjekt
Superlative	2. Steigerungsstufe / Superlativ
Tense	Zeitform
Third conditional	*If*-Satz vom Typ 3
Uncountables	Nicht zählbare Wörter
Verb	Zeitwort / Verb

Grammar index

Grammatikregister